The Square Root of You

The Square Root of You

REDISCOVERING YOUR POTENTIAL, PASSIONS, AND PURPOSE

Ron Schlitt

Copyright © 2017 by Ron Schlitt
All rights reserved. No part of this publication may be reproduced, distributed, or transmitted in any form or by any means, including photocopying, recording, or other electronic or mechanical methods, without the prior written permission of the author, except in the case of brief quotations embodied in critical reviews and certain other noncommercial uses permitted by copyright law.
ISBN-13: 9781519196729
ISBN-10: 1519196725
Library of Congress Control Number: 2017914202
CreateSpace Independent Publishing Platform
North Charleston, South Carolina

Dedicated to Dianne, Jory, and Jayme

Contents

Introduction ix

Chapter 1	The Selfless Act of Self 1
Chapter 2	The Games We Play with Names 5
Chapter 3	We Got Potential All Wrong 11
Chapter 4	The Ancient Story That Keeps Repeating 19
Chapter 5	You Have but One, Not Nine 29
Chapter 6	Not Failure, but Feedback 37
Chapter 7	What's Belief Got to Do with It? 45
Chapter 8	Two Little Words That Make a Big Difference ... 49
Chapter 9	More or Less 55
Chapter 10	Excuse Me, but Your Label Is Sticking Out 61
Chapter 11	Size Does Matter 69
Chapter 12	Straight A's 77
Chapter 13	Treasure Hunting 83
Chapter 14	Your Turn 91

Sample Narrative 99

Acknowledgments 101

Suggested Resources 103

**Discovering your potential
leads to developing your passions,
which leads to determining your purpose.**

Introduction

You have a calling and a mission in this life! What does that statement do to you when you hear it? Do you agree? Disagree? Do you think it, but your actions show that you do not believe it? Are you one of the many who at some point begin to wonder if life just happens by chance and luck? That some people just happen to win the lottery of defined purpose, but you haven't even bought a ticket?

I was compelled to write this book after years of trying to explain to others what I actually do for a living. Trying to put into a job title what I do so others can easily understand my role has always been a challenge. Although I have helped people figure out how they are wired, I am not an electrician. I assist teams when things are stuck, but I am not a plumber. I get people and groups to build their future, but I am not a carpenter. I have the privilege of getting people to put two and two together, but I am not a mathematician. And so I go through life often searching to get that one job title that defines me and gives me my identity and purpose. I wonder how many others find themselves in a similar quandary. I stopped trying to give myself a job title and now explain my role with the following sentence: I help individuals, teams, and organizations discover the realities of their potential in order for it to be released.

Having done exactly that for most of my career, I have discovered what I believe to be the three main questions I hear most individuals have when they strive to move from "doing" to "being."

1. Who am I? (potential)
2. How do I belong? (passions)
3. Where can I have the greatest impact? (purpose)

I suspect you are presently asking yourself these questions (in one form or another). You are likely on a road called discovery. Life is the process of discovery, and that is what makes living so amazing. If we never discovered, this life we live would be barren and desolate like most of the planets in our universe. Humans have a built-in need and desire to discover, and I am convinced that it needs to start in the discovery of who we are, how we belong, and where we have the opportunities for the greatest impact on others. Basically we need to understand the square root of ourselves. A square root is a number that when multiplied by itself gives you the original number—the truest measure. We have heard for years of people going back to their "roots" and of groups returning to their "grass roots." Now there's all the talk of their DNA, which is primarily about their unique genetic makeup, yet few of us figure out who we are at our own core or root. A study of the most successful people will show you that they can describe to you exactly who they are and who they are not, and within that they have a freedom we all seek.

Discovering your potential leads to developing your passions, which leads to determining your purpose.

The pages that follow are presented as a series of essays that are meant to interconnect. I have one question to ask of you to start, and that is this:

Will you commit to going beyond just reading some words on a page and seriously muse and answer one rediscovery question I will pose at the end of each chapter? If you answer yes and follow through to the last chapter, you will be able to weave together all your answers and discover the square root of you—the rediscovery of your potential, passions, and purpose.

The intention of this process follows along the lines of the Quaker tradition of a "clearness committee." It is the process by which a group refrains from giving you advice, judgments, criticisms, or solutions but instead spends time simply asking open and honest questions to help one discover truth. Treat the following pages and questions as your own "clearness committee" that guides you to discover your beauty and genius.

Clarity often comes when we finally hear and listen to what lies beneath in our core. If some of the questions sound similar and your answers seem to repeat in another chapter, that is a good thing, and you are simply hitting something that you need to pay attention to. The final assignment given in these pages is a space for you to write the narrative of who you are, where you belong, and the impact you will make. When you do that, you find clarity.

So here is your first question: Are you ready to do some honest self-reflection?

You can be yourself without pursuing yourself. Have you ever seen a dog chase his own tail? He just runs in circles.

—Criss Jami, *Killosophy*

CHAPTER 1

The Selfless Act of Self

The most unselfish thing you can do is to spend time and energy on getting to know yourself to the core. It may sound a little selfish and narcissistic, but the truth is that understanding *you* can be the greatest gift you give others. On the flip side, not being authentically *you* is fraught with believing the lies you and others tell, and you become more self-centered as you try to be everything to everyone.

The goal of well-roundedness always ends in failure and frustration not only for you but also for others. The need for power and control, having to be in charge and good in every aspect of your life, leaves little or nothing for anyone else to play a role in your daily life, except to feed your ego and insatiable hunger for affirmation. Have you ever noticed how selfish people bring out the selfishness in others? The opposite is just as true—unselfish acts bring out the generosity of others.

If we truly could find the elixir of how to be well rounded, we would not need another soul to be or do anything other than to applaud our successes. We have all met this delusional individual, and that person soon becomes isolated and the least-liked individual in the organization. The person's lack of honest self-perception becomes a never-ending hunger of expectations that can never be fully satisfied. It is sheer hypocrisy if we live a life other than our own authentic self.

All the studies around the best of the best contain the same two conclusions: they know who they are and work at being that as often as possible, and secondly, they know who they are not and manage around it. And the way they manage around that is by unselfishly allowing others to be themselves, which empowers the others as well as the person doing the allowing. The fact that the best of the best know themselves so well not only provides freedom for them, but it also causes them to completely rely on others to contribute their talents and gifts for the greater good. Success is achieved in collaboration with others—the selfless act of self.

The people I have met who understand this concept of authenticity are able to describe in detail how they can most productively contribute—how they can be generative (giving life to not only themselves but others). They find their potential, passions, and purpose by the gift of giving of themselves.

Not unlike an owner's manual that comes with the products you buy and begin to use, so it should be that you create a manual about yourself. A good owner's manual not only contains the specifications of how something is built and designed but also how best to use the product to gain maximum benefit and purpose. It points to the strengths of the product and cautions about areas of weakness—which could be things it was never designed to do. Successful and content people who are comfortable in their own skin have somehow figured out an owner's manual about themselves. When we meet these people, they have a way of reaching into our lives, and the reason they impact us is because they are not trying to be us—they leave that job up to us.

It sounds so easy in theory, but it's so hard to do in practice. Society has trained us to strive and be strong in everything—never showing signs of weakness. Pride, ego, control, power, greed, fame, fortune, and expectations of others all get in the way, which launches us back into the temptation of being a one-person show (the loneliest number of all).

If you picked up this book thinking it was all about you, you might end up surprised at how much it is about others. When you really begin to get honest about yourself, you begin to look at others differently, and frankly that changes everything. When we give self to others, we become more of whom we really are, and that is simply called authenticity.

I can stick artificial flowers on this tree that will not flower, or I can create the conditions in which the tree is likely to flower naturally. I may have to wait longer for my real flowers but they are the only true ones.

—John Fowles, *The Aristos*

Rediscovery

What parts of your daily life do you joyfully and willingly give to others?

_____
_____
_____
_____
_____
_____
_____

"It's poor judgement," said Grandpa, "to call anything by a name. We don't know what a hobgoblin or a vampire or a troll is. Could be lots of things. You can't heave them into categories with labels and say they'll act one way or another. That'd be silly. They're people. People who do things. Yes, that's the way to put it: people who *do* things."

—Ray Bradbury, *The October Country*, "The Man Upstairs"

CHAPTER 2

The Games We Play with Names

What's in a name? We can't seem to go to any social gathering without one of the very first questions asked when starting a conversation being this: "So, what do you do?" Likely this serves as any easy entry point into breaking the ice with someone. And for the socially awkward, it is a technique taught by lifestyle coaches to help us introverts of the world manage the nervousness of engaging in conversation with strangers. The question serves a couple of purposes other than just a way to break the ice. Firstly, it allows us to form some type of judgment based on the information we have gathered over the years from previous encounters we have had from others with similar titles. Secondly, it gives us the opportunity to measure our "society status" and ranking based on our personal securities, insecurities, beliefs, and biases in relation to one another.

There was a day, believe it or not, that there was no need to ask that question. In the early days of small villages in medieval Europe, the practice called "byname" began. It was a way of helping others distinguish one Stephen from all the other Stephens who may have lived in the same village. The result may have looked something like this: "Oh, that is Stephen, John's son." The translation became, "Meet Stephen Johnson." A "byname" was based on an individual's occupation, status, or area of residence. Mr. Farmer likely was a farmer while Mr. Baker probably ran the local bakery. Mr. Field likely owned the field on the edge of town that everyone knew about and used as a point of reference for direction. And so on and so on it went.

We no longer refer to our last names as "bynames," but we call them "surnames," and our surnames do not necessarily describe what we do for a living, where we come from, or our status in the community. With a last name like mine—Schlitt—I am most grateful for living in this age and not somewhere in medieval Europe.

Today, because we do not use "bynames," we somehow have to resort to other ways to figure out who someone is, and we ask the question "So, what do you do?" Whether or not we have a favorable or unfavorable understanding and acceptance of the response we hear, we begin to label one another based on job title alone. What comes to mind when you hear "I am a used-car salesman," "I am a dentist," "I am a psychologist," "I am a TV evangelist," or "I am a stay-at-home parent"? You make a judgment or begin to label each person, don't you? You are no different from the rest of us when it comes to jumping to some conclusion about who someone is simply by the title of that person's chosen career. We all do it, and I suspect it is the way in which our minds try to make sense of the world around us.

I do not fault you. It is in most cases an efficient way for us to absorb and process what could be a huge amount of information in a very short and concise way. Although efficient, it carries a very low percentage of accuracy about the things that really matter—like how good those people are at their craft (their potential), what they care about (their passions), and where they are likely to have the greatest impact (their purpose).

Today, it is almost impossible to hear a surname and know exactly what career that person has. There are a few exceptions to this rule, and that falls into the study of aptronyms—names that match the occupation. A few fun examples are that Lord Brain was a neurologist; Larry Speaks was a former spokesman for President Reagan; astronaut Buzz Aldrin's mother's maiden name was Marion Moon; Lake Speed was a NASCAR driver; Dr. David Toothaker practiced dentistry in Arkansas; and, according to one website all about aptronyms, Dr. Coffin, Dr. Fearing, Dr. Sorrow, Dr. Pray, and Dr. Death (pronounced "Deeth") should either change their surnames or profession.

I used to hate the question "What do you do for a living?" because I knew that the person asking was simply looking for a one-word job title. Not having a traditional career, I would use paragraph upon paragraph trying to describe and explain what I did on a daily basis, and I would get the same glaze of confusion from everyone. I eventually gave in and told everyone, "My name is Ron Schlitt, and I am a plumber!" With a last name like Schlitt, I made a determination during grade school recess that I had three choices about my last name: I could eventually change it, I could hide it as much as possible, or I could find a way to make it an advantage for me. Today I have a lot of fun with my last name and embrace the opportunities to put others at ease quickly by using creative expressions with the name "Schlitt." After all Schlitt happens.

When we move from a descriptive name to an abstract label, we are more distant with the core reality of our truest self, and we begin to water down our best self and what that self could become. In most of our cultural settings, the title we carry or that is given to us holds far more importance than any of our capacities and passions, and we begin to behave in ways that are less and less in line with who we truly are.

How much better would our social interactions be if we bypassed titles and all the social judgments that come with our preconceived perceptions of matching the "who" with the "what" that is based on one word—plumber, electrician, doctor, janitor, barista, cabbie, pilot, and so on?

Can you imagine what amazing conversations you could have if you asked or were asked, "What do you love to do that generates life in you and those around you?" You may hear the lawyer speak of a passion for ensuring the less fortunate get fair justice in an unjust world. You may hear the doctor speak of bringing a small piece of dignity to a suffering patient in a hospice house. You may hear of the houseparent who passionately invests in the next generation by volunteering at the local school's after-hours reading program. And what about hearing the politician speak of a passion to ensure our society stays a safe and welcoming place for the disenfranchised and mentally ill citizens on our streets? Now that is a social function I would love to be invited to. That is a community that would inspire, give us all hope, and break down the stereotypes of labeling one another by career title. Our thinking would be stretched, and our view of one another's differences would change so the differences would be seen not as negatives but as positives. We would likely begin to stop hiding inside a box generating a bunch of excuses about what we can't do. Instead, we would willingly step on top of the box and describe with passion who we are and the mission we aspire to.

Sounds like an amazing conversation, but my suspicions are that very few of us could do this with strangers because we have not taken any time to reflect upon what it is we ourselves do that we *love* to do. Most of us would need to trick our minds for a moment and drop the "title" we carry. We would need to ignore the pride or shame we have regarding ourselves in our comparison to others in the room based on our status within society tied to some title. Sometimes I sit back and simply observe social gatherings and interactions and see all of us trying to be magicians. We carefully set the stage and cautiously pick our words to give the other person an illusion that what we do is indeed who we are. The problem is that the conclusion of the illusion in that case is left up to the audience and its members' interpretation as they see and understand it, and the illusion may not have the effect the magician expected. If you tell me that you are a used-car salesman, it is I who determines the outcome of the illusion—not you. But if you tell me that you love assisting people to make wise choices in transportation within their lifestyle needs and budget, I have no other illusion than the fact you love what you do for others. I now know not only what you do, but also I know why you do it, and that is no longer an illusion. It's the truth.

Now it is your turn, and this is a chance to gain some clarity. In the question that follows, take some time to write out a statement or two that goes beyond a simple job or career title. If you do, I am sure your conversations with others will change, and engaging conversations will naturally happen time and time again.

<u>Rediscovery</u>

What do you love to do that generates life in you and others?

_____
_____
_____
_____
_____
_____

Every day that we fail to live out the maximum of our potentials we kill the Shakespeare, Dante, Homer, Christ which is in us.

—Henry Miller

CHAPTER 3

We Got Potential All Wrong

When we invite guests to our house, they normally are asked if they would like to come over to "the Schlitt house" for dinner. Those who are not aware of our last name take a little longer to register an affirmative response, but they are normally guaranteed great food, good wine, and a few laughs intertwined with some engaging conversation. During the summer months, we add one more surprise. Around sunset, when the light of dusk still prevails, we usher our guests out to the backyard. With wide eyes and likely a bit of mistrust, they head out the back door with us, past the patio and the comfortable outdoor furniture, and onto the grass while we walk to the far corner of the yard. We stand facing a plot of dirt in the garden that has a plant that truly looks more like a dandelion weed than something anyone would plant, let alone tend and take care of. More than one comment has been directed to us about the importance of regularly weeding our flower bed. And so we stand in a semicircle, shoulder to shoulder, staring at a leafy green plant. I break the awkward silence with a statement that sounds a bit like this: "You are about to witness a mind-blowing event where you will see what true potential in action looks like." And then the magic happens, often with our doubting guests suddenly falling to their knees in amazement and awe to get a closer look as they observe potential released. As if kneeling to the flower gods in honor of what they have just experienced, they "oh" and "ah" for the next several minutes at this spectacle of nature and creation.

Tucked away in the far corner of our backyard under a small tree is an *Oenothera acaulis aurea*, better known in common English as a moonflower. This small plant, which often is mistaken for a dandelion because of its green leaves, blooms almost every night as the sun sets and darkness begins to fall. Tiny buds bloom before your eyes as if you were watching some time-lapse photography on a BBC *Planet Earth* video. But what you get to marvel at is the fact that this isn't time-lapse photography but a real-time event of a few seconds, during which you get to admire a beautiful yellow flower fully bloom. Simply amazing.

If the moonflower were to simply get itself to the stage of a bud on a stem, we would stand staring at potential *reached*. But the fact that we can see that potential be *released* tells me that we have too often described human potential incorrectly. We have gotten it wrong for years in corporations, education, families, and sports.

How often do we hear someone describing others by saying, "I want them to reach their potential" or "They just never seem to reach their potential"? We base our performance-management systems around reaching potential and reward or punishment based on the result. We shouldn't be concerned with getting people, coworkers, team members, or even ourselves to *reach* potential, but with an eye to examples such as the moonflower, we should be concerning ourselves with *releasing* our potential.

Potential *reached* and potential *released* are actually two very different things. Reaching our potential is simply getting to the starting line. All our training, education, and preparation, along with emotions, desires, and dreams, are pent up together and ready to just do it. It is like being a runner in the starting blocks; all the elements are combined and ready for such a time as this. But it isn't until the gun sounds and there is action on the part of the runner that we see potential reached converted to potential released. Isn't that what we hope for in our careers and daily life? We want to get out of the starting blocks and into the race, doing what we were created and born to do.

We go off to school, put in our time, and begin to hone a few skills. Then the wait begins for that chance to show the world why and what we have been created to do and be. But sadly, very few of us somehow figure out how to realize the potential we have, so we lie in wait for years, and soon the sun sets, and the bud stays a bud and never releases the power of being a flower. And your company loses, your team loses, and you lose.

What truly amazes me is that so few of us can describe what our potential released would actually look like. We appear to have become trained by society to believe that circumstances totally dictate the release of our potential. If that is what we believe, then why do so few people place themselves into the very environments that can allow circumstances to facilitate the realization of the desires from within? I am convinced the reason they do not consciously place themselves in those environments is because they have never stopped to figure out what their potential released would actually look like in accordance with actual daily activities and actions. Instead, they complain about never getting the break they need, so they live in the world of "if only."

Imagine a Lamborghini sitting in your garage. Looks great with the newly waxed race car–red paint and with chrome that shines as bright as silver ever could. Makes for a great picture for you and your friends to stand beside and take selfies. There's so much potential, but that car was not manufactured to sit in a garage for pictures and "if onlys." It was created to fulfill the purpose of driving on a highway built for speed and acceleration. Each of us has a Lamborghini in our potential, but we store it in a garage of excuses and blame it on circumstances.

Before you think I am making this sound all too easy and that you alone are to blame for your potential not being released, I am not! I get it! It is hard! That is why so few of us get to experience the fullness of potential released. Life happens. Responsibilities creep in. Bosses get insecure. Budgets get cut. Layoffs and terminations occur. I can't guarantee many things, but I can guarantee that those things will happen. But have you taken the time to list the details around the ideal environment and the types of people you need to be surrounded by in order for you to be the best you can be and release your potential?

For years I felt underutilized and disillusioned with a whole bunch of pent-up potential lying dormant within. In the corporate world, I would have been characterized as a disengaged employee—lots of potential but little or no outlet for others to see the very best of me. It was no fault of my employer. I was doing the job I was hired to do, and it certainly was not the responsibility of the company to cater to me by redesigning a job description for my selfish needs and ambitions. The problem lay more or less with me because I couldn't describe with any kind of detail what my released potential would look like and how that would benefit the company. At best, I could describe in vague generalities a task or issue that I was passionate about, but the details remained a mystery to others. It wasn't until I hit a wall due to pure boredom and frustration that I forced myself to stop and reflect on what the core of my potential actually was and how that would appear if released. Looking back now, I wonder whether, if I had never hit the wall, I would ever have given myself the permission to explore and be truthful with myself and accept who I am, who I am not, and what I need to be more of.

I do not think for even one second that everyone needs to get to a crisis point in order to figure this out. I would encourage everyone to not wait for a crisis since the quality of decision-making tends to go down during such a time. We make clearer observations and better judgments and decisions, especially about ourselves, when we are not at a crisis point. I seem to spend time listening to people who are incredibly successful in the eyes of others but who nevertheless feel stifled, like a flower bud that just cannot bloom. I often hear this: "I wish I would have figured this out about myself in my twenties and not waited until now." Or I hear this: "I need to get this into the hands of my kids so they don't waste years trying to figure this stuff out like I did."

Almost all of these individuals likely would be in the same career but would have played a more significant role and for a longer period of time had they been able to describe their potential in more detail and then aligned that with the activities within that career. It would have likely meant a minor adjustment here and there that would have made all the difference earlier on. I once heard a coach say, "If you don't think small things matter, try losing a game by one point" (more about that in another chapter). Hollywood movies lead us to believe that career changes for disengaged individuals are some huge life-altering shifts in which true potential is realized only after selling everything, trekking off with a backpack to some faraway land, and saving a nation. Makes for great entertainment, but it just does not reflect the truth about life.

Perhaps that is one of the first hurdles or roadblocks you need to get over. It isn't a huge, insurmountable, life-altering change that you make overnight. It starts with you answering truthfully and in some detail what your unique passions would look like when released. Dream a bit. Trust your instincts. Speak truth to yourself.

Rediscovery

What would your passions look like if released?

_____
_____
_____
_____
_____
_____
_____

You see the giant and the shepherd in the Valley of Elah and your eye is drawn to the man with the sword and shield and the glittering armor. But so much of what is beautiful and valuable in the world comes from the shepherd, who has more strength and purpose than we ever imagine.

—Malcolm Gladwell, *David and Goliath*

CHAPTER 4

The Ancient Story That Keeps Repeating

You may never have read the ancient text as it was originally written thousands of years ago, but I am pretty sure you have heard the story, or at least some form of reference to it. You may have heard it in school, perhaps at work around the water cooler, on a news report, or maybe even in a church. Entire books have been written around the story, and it is often referred to within our legal and corporate structures. We look to this story for inspiration and hope. You've likely even imagined being the main character and hero of the story, especially when you were in some kind of battle that appeared to have someone else with an unfair advantage. Maybe it was a fight in which you felt ill equipped and full of self-doubt, and others' voices were placing their bets on the foe you battled.

The age-old story I am talking about has two main characters: a small underdog with the name David and a giant and champion with the name Goliath. It is about an epic battle where the high stakes of win or lose are everything. It includes a king and a bunch of supporting characters who sit on the sidelines giving all kinds of advice and opinions, most of which are unhelpful and based purely on perception, judgment, insecurity, and fear.

I will not recite the entire story to you, as I am sure that if you have been on this earth for any length of time, you have heard it at least a few times. Many others have written about David and Goliath much better than I could ever do. A quick Internet search will provide you many great reads if you wish to study in further detail. For now, however, I want to look at this ancient story from a slightly different perspective and look at the cast of characters from a different set of eyes. I am making the assumption you know the main plot and end result of this story, but in case you don't or need a reminder, here is the shortest version I can think of to set the stage for the remainder of this chapter. Small shepherd boy David meets giant Goliath. David, the underdog, kills the champion fighter, Goliath. David saves the nation of Israel from captivity and eventually becomes the king of the Jewish nation.

There are a few things contained in this story I find intriguing when I look at it from a strengths and weaknesses or, better put, a potentials and limitations perspective. I freely admit to you that I have taken some liberties in what the thoughts and conversations might have been that day, which are not contained in the original text of the Bible.

First, David, the underdog, seems to be completely underequipped and barely armed to enter any kind of warfare against a fully supplied foe like Goliath. David was underfunded, lacked human battle experience, and did not appear to be any kind of threat in anyone's eyes. Everyone doubted David except David himself. Why did he believe what we could not? Was he just delusional, like most teenagers are in their imaginations of what they can be and do? Was he just that insecure little brother striving to prove a point and be everything to everyone, and if he met failure, at least he could be acclaimed as a martyr? As I read that story, I come to the conclusion that David wasn't some teenager with delusional thoughts but that he knew exactly what he was and what he was not. When King Saul finally determined that his army had no more hope of defeating the challenge from its enemy to fight its champion, Goliath, along came this kid with a homemade leather pouch attached to two strings—what we call a slingshot.

With huge consequences to be suffered if his representative lost, the king finally agreed to let this sheep tender enter into battle against some guy who had been taunting and trash-talking them for days. What was King Saul thinking? Can you imagine being one of his soldiers and hearing that this kid was going to go out and represent the army on its behalf? I would question any leader like that, and if I had any thoughts of who was delusional, I know my money would have been on the idea that King Saul had lost his freaking mind.

And then Saul did something we all do. He gave David his own suit of armor and his personal royal sword, because after all, if he was in the fight, that is what he would use. If it was good for him, it must have been good for everyone else. In other words, he was building in David a "mini-me." So what did David do? He put the suit on and tried swinging the sword. He couldn't move! He couldn't hit anything! He almost fell over trying! He realized almost instantly that this just did not feel right, and this was the road to sure loss and disaster, and the nation of Israel would be no longer. The restriction caused by trying to be Saul and not David would not be an advantage but a costly disadvantage, or otherwise put, not a strength but a weakness, not a potential but a limitation.

Who in your life has been a King Saul? Such a person might have had good intentions and was probably trying to help and protect you, but the person was actually stifling your potential by telling you that if you did it that person's way, it would be better for you because that is what had worked best for him or her. And if that person could be successful, the only way you would be successful would be to be just like that person. So you gave in and tried but failed, and you tried again and again, and you failed again and again. Before long you doubted you had any potential, and you began to live in the land of limitations that never became anything more than a place of frustration and disappointment.

We "Saul" on those around us. As parents, we "Saul" on our kids. As teachers, we "Saul" on our students. As friends, we "Saul" on our pals. As spouses, we "Saul" on our beloveds. And as bosses, we "Saul" on our staff.

Your suit of armor is built for you—custom made and not designed as a one-size-fits-all piece. King Saul's armor didn't fit David, and it won't fit you. Let's give Saul a bit of grace in that he did try what he thought was best, and in the end he did let David be David on the battlefield.

We also need to acknowledge that David did at least try on the suit from King Saul to see if he could indeed function in that armor. Maybe it was an option. Maybe it could work. He would have never known had he not at least tried a little pilot project. We all need to at least try a few things to see if we experience success or failure; we may discover something new, enriching, and exciting. Let's not forget, however, that a pilot project should be tested when the stakes are low and not a matter of life and death. Pro golfers will tell you that the time to try something new in your swing is not while you are in the midst of a championship match but rather when you are on the practice range.

What of the enemy—Goliath himself? He taunted, trash-talked, and jeered at David that day. He asked out loud if this was some kind of joke that this scrawny excuse of a human being was going to fight someone who was as great a champion as himself. How many Goliaths do you face daily who make judgments about your abilities based solely on an outward appearance? Goliath had no previous knowledge of what this kid had done in the past with his choice of weapon, the slingshot. Was he aware that David had killed a bear and a lion to protect his flock? And wouldn't the flock he belonged to, Israel, be an even more important flock than actual bleating sheep?

Goliath wasn't the only naysayer that day. David originally went to the battlefield on the instructions of his dad to bring his brothers some food and to report back on how they were doing. Instead of open arms and gratefulness at seeing his little brother and what gifts he had brought, the oldest brother, Eliab, accused him of conceit, wickedness, and only wanting to watch the battle. Even those we think are in our corner may not see our differences as an advantage.

David faced more than one person telling him he was crazy, unskilled, and in possession of no potential to do anything more than chase a few sheep around a field that day. Everyone saw David through the perceptions of their own eyes and their own understanding and experiences, and this masked any potential as mere limitations in their eyes. This was the viewpoint of all except for David himself.

Had David listened and believed what he heard that day, Goliath would have won, and history would be different than we know it today. But David trusted what he knew to be true. He knew what he could do. He knew what he could not do. He knew what he loved and yearned for. At some point you need to be a David and stand up after weighing the words of others. You need to allow what you know to be the truth to guide and direct you toward what you know about yourself: your experiences, your desires, your yearnings and cravings, the things you love, and the things you look forward to doing.

This brings me to the next fascinating part of the story. David did not stand on the sidelines waiting and hoping to get noticed and invited to the battle. He saw an opportunity that would allow all his potential to be released into something powerful and potent. He heard the call and approached the giant. David had to get in the face of King Saul, raise his hand, and say, "I'll do it!" He volunteered with all his past skills, knowledge, abilities, passions, and potential, and so must you. If you want to release your potential, you are going to have to be confident enough to at least raise your hand the next time an opportunity arises—an opportunity that you crave and that produces an excitement that almost cannot be contained. If you think that one day somehow the world is going to awaken from its slumber and take notice of you standing on the sidelines with all that potential, and that it then will invite you into the battle against some giants you know you can defeat, you are likely to become very disappointed. The world just doesn't tend to work that way. If you want to do battle with the giants you know you can defeat—giants whom you were created to fight better than anyone else—you will need to do like David and position yourself. What a sad story it would be to end with the words "Too bad he didn't get into the battle. He had so much potential." Positioning means getting yourself into the right place at the right time and then putting that hand up, saying, "I can do it. I have the right capabilities, passions, and potential. If you want to see the very best of me, and if you want me to help us win, then put me in the game. I am good to go."

People often tell me that they never get a break and aren't lucky enough—like someone else they cite—to be in the right place at the right time. When talking with the so-called lucky ones, I discover that getting that so-called lucky break required action on their part. Had they not placed themselves in the proper position or stance to take advantage of the opportunity when it presented itself, they would never have gotten the so-called lucky break. It barely ever comes down to luck; it comes down to who positioned themselves better. David's brothers and any other soldier had the same opportunity as David that day to be the hero, but it was David who positioned himself in front of King Saul. Was he really the guy who got the lucky break? Much like David, you may need to convince and tell others of your potential. They likely don't know what excites you or the things you crave to do. After hearing what you have to say, they will make their own assessment about you based on their limited knowledge, perceptions, and insecurities. So look to those places and times when positioning yourself and speaking up will make the difference.

How did David know with such confidence that even though he was totally underpowered in weaponry by battle standards and so unprotected in shepherd's clothing, he could defeat a superficially superior warrior? Did he simply get an adrenalin high that boosted his self-confidence, or was there something else? Did he somehow just attain some unknown and undiscovered skill? Was there some higher power—namely, God—that took over and possessed his body? Most of us when reading this story miss the point that David had years of training, practice, and skill development before the day he met Goliath. The day of battle with Goliath wasn't the first time David had gone to the creek bank and picked a few stones to place in his pouch. It wasn't the first time he had ever twirled a rock and sling around his head at warp speed. He didn't just get lucky and accidentally somehow know exactly when to let go of one string—or even which one to let go of—so that the projectile would travel at bullet speed and enter perfectly into the one open, vulnerable area of Goliath's forehead. No, that was not a one-time fluke. David had practiced for years when tending sheep in the fields where no other humans likely even saw what he could do. No wonder everyone that day was suspicious and sure he was nuts to think he could win that fight. They had never once seen him kill anything. All they knew was that he slept in the field by some docile sheep. And it is no wonder David himself had to tell them he was the guy for the job, because all they saw was a kid holding what today we call a slingshot. David certainly was an "overnight success"—after about fifteen years of hard work.

What about the five stones he picked up in the creek that day? How did he know which were the best ones to use to have the best velocity and flight path? He knew which ones and how many to pick because he had practiced for a game-day situation more than once. He had experienced failure and success, and he knew without a doubt which stones would be best. Even though he only needed one stone—thankfully for the army of Israel, he did it with the first one—I have no doubt that in his mind he knew from past experience that if he missed with the first one, he would not have time to run back and get more. He had more to offer if need be. It was what he knew of himself that gave him such passionate confidence in his ability to slay the giant—what none of us would have believed by just looking at this scrawny little kid. Yup, David was a fifteen-year overnight success!

I know the story is often told as a miracle, but I would argue that it wasn't actually a miracle in the way we often present it to be. I think the bigger miracle would have been if David had put on King Saul's armor and defeated the giant Goliath with King Saul's sword—basically winning the battle by using tools and wearing something he never had worn before that would have handicapped his true potential. The fact is that David had prepared for years prior to the battle, knew who he was, and even better, knew who he wasn't. He stayed true to who he was—the genuine shepherd boy David, and when the time came, he stood up and said, "I can do that."

Hear the call—run to the giant!

Rediscovery

Where do you need to position yourself so your potential can be realized and released?

_____
_____
_____
_____
_____
_____
_____

The real me isn't the person I describe, no the real me is the me revealed by my actions.

—Malcolm Gladwell, *Blink*

CHAPTER 5

You Have but One, Not Nine

All dogs go to heaven! According to the Hollywood movie that is titled the same, one is led to believe that dogs go to heaven and cats not so much. I guess that is OK, as apparently cats have nine lives, so they basically get a bunch of "do-overs" anyway. I don't want to offend "cat people," so I will refrain from making any jokes about the feline world, but I am admittedly a "dog person."

How did the expression "a cat has nine lives" actually originate? There are a number of theories as to the origin of this expression, but I think we can all agree that cats have a knack for dodging death, and when falling from high places, they seem to not only survive but also simply walk away with an arrogant and superior strut as if to say, "You mortal humans, I meant to do that—now worship me!" The reason cats almost always land on their feet is because of what science refers to as a "righting reflex"—basically they can twist around very quickly when dropped from a high place. I do not recommend you try to see if you have a righting reflex.

So if we humans do not have nine lives, then we need to do the very best with the one that we do have. And what happens when we don't live the life we are leading others to believe we are living? In the movie *Wild*

Hogs, a bunch of rather disillusioned friends, when going through their midlife crises, hit the road on motorcycles that for the most part do not fit their mainstream corporate images. Upon meeting up with a real motorcycle gang, they are accused of simply being a bunch of "posers"—being something they are not, leading a double life, and not living authentically.

I accuse all but a very few of us of being posers. We are guilty of trying to live a life that others expect. Many of us are living today from the "outside in" when to be at our best we should be living from the "inside out." When we live to the expectations others have of us, such a life is not congruent with our genuine self, and we don't land on our feet with the prowess of a feline. If you have ever tried to be what others want you to be, you know exactly what it means to live from the "outside in." Whether it is because you are trying to fit in or trying to be accepted, liked, loved, well thought of, or harmonious or whether you are trying to climb a social ladder or trying to get corporate acclaim, if you are not doing it out of your core authenticity, you are a poser.

How many other people's lives have you tried to live? We need to be truthful about ourselves before we can even think of being truthful, real, and authentic with others. "Fake it till you make it!" may buy you a bit of time, but eventually faking it will not end well for you. We most often head directly into disappointment, disillusionment, and failure when we live someone else's life and not our own. I am talking about a selfish, self-centered posture here. I am referring to the truth that when we try to be someone else, we cheat not only ourselves of being our best, but we also selfishly do not allow the other person to be the best he or she can be either.

"Fake it till you make it" more accurately is "Fake it till you break it." You end up breaking trust. You break confidence. You break careers. You break self-esteem. You break personal health. You break relationships. And you break community. Not so long ago, I was working with a corporate team, and we were discussing truth and authenticity in relation to engagement and careers. One young lady in her midthirties spoke of her previous position in sales. She spoke of the awards she had won consistently as a top performer and the perks that went with the status. She then went on to tell us how she hated the job and knew that although she was good at it, she was faking it the entire time because it wasn't who she really was. This sales journey ended for her abruptly one day when she was rushed to the hospital after suffering a heart attack. She maintains to this day that trying to live a life from the "outside in" at work was literally killing her. She is grateful that she is now in a career that is true to who she was created to be and living an "inside out" life and loving it.

Who you are is inclusive of the activities that get you reenergized, excited, and engaged. It is contagious. It includes the things you find yourself daydreaming about and the things you internally know bring you joy.

Sigmund Freud may have been onto something when he stated, "When making decisions of minor importance, I have always found it advantageous to consider all the pros and cons. In vital matters, however, such as the choice of a mate or a profession, the decision should come from the unconscious, from somewhere within ourselves. In the important decisions of personal life, we should be governed, I think, by the deep inner needs of our nature."

As children we are born with an almost insatiable curiosity to explore, invest, and dream. We are full of hope. We start kindergarten with this enthusiasm of becoming who we are and what we love to do. In just a few very short years, we have conformed to the system, and the curiosity we once had wanes to a suppressed feeling, and the childhood curiosity rarely resurfaces. The fire inside dwindles to less than a flicker, and midlife becomes a daze of conformity to expectations of those who seem to believe they have a perfect plan for our lives. Some are lucky to find that upon retirement the fire reignites. Curiosity resurfaces, and the adventure of becoming begins once again. For most of us, life is like the front cover of a book, full of anticipation and hopeful expectations. The back cover is like the end of the journey we started. We have somehow lost all the goodness of the pages in between those two covers. The pages in between should be the bulk of the time we spend on this earth touching lives and living authentically. How exciting would it be to have each page be not just a blur of words but be full of the adventure of being ourselves and not just doing that which doesn't fit with being ourselves?

Could that be why, when we ask a young child what he or she wants to be when grown up, the response is never this: "I don't know. Let me get back to you on that." No! Without hesitation, the child plops out an answer that is full of excitement and anticipation. And when children tell us that they want to be superheroes, we laugh to ourselves and chalk it up to childish impossibilities. But if you truly want to see what may be behind their response and a possible window to their future potential, try adding a follow-up question. You just might be surprised by what their answers reveal about the inner needs of their nature. Ask this: "Why do you want superpowers, and what would you do with them? An answer like "help poor people" might come from a future activist. "Fight evil people" might come from a future law enforcement official. "Go to other planets and fly spaceships" might come from a future scientist.

This came true to me many years ago when I brought my son to my business. At the time, it was swarming with staff and clients as he held my hand and as I walked around showing him all the cool things we had going on. It was a 100 percent people-centered organization, and the product was human resources. At the end of the tour as we sat in my office, I said what many a dad might say: "Son, one day this may all be yours."

He surprised me with his answer. "Yeah, but I would probably turn it into a science lab or something like that." Needless to say, I chuckled out loud because what I was doing was the furthest thing from a science lab you could ever imagine. So where is he now? He has just recently graduated with a degree in chemistry and is about to enter into teaching science nerds for the foreseeable future. I guess he knew something I didn't all those years ago.

Then there is my daughter, who spent countless hours as a young child placing bandages and tensor wraps around not only her stuffed toys but me as well. Today she finds herself preparing for a career in occupational therapy.

There is genius inside each one of us, and we keep suppressing it when we stop listening to that internal voice. When we heed the words of others who want us to live the life they wish they had lived, we begin to live that "poser" life. We begin to believe that living a life other than our own is somehow better, we begin to live life from the "outside in," and we end up wasting that one life we have. Then we wonder why a catlike righting reflex does not kick in.

All your successes and all your failures are clues to who you truly are. I understand why many of us do not want to face some of the realities of those findings about ourselves. When we eliminate the mystery and reveal the truth, it carries with it responsibility and authority. If it stays a mystery, we can always brush it aside and make excuses, but that which is revealed requires action on our parts. If we are suppressing and ignoring our inner needs and nature, we are prisoners to the society of others who are trying to mold and craft us into what they want us to be and not who we need to be. We are held captive by the chains of expectations that cannot be met, the hopes that fall short, and the dreams that disappoint. But when you discover who you are and, just as importantly, who you are not, and you begin to live within that acceptance, you truly experience the freedom of living an "inside out" life. Transparency and authenticity that reveal the real you allow everyone to see the best of you—your beauty and genius. And you ultimately live the one life you have, full of potential, passion, and purpose.

Benjamin Franklin has been credited with this saying: "Be yourself because everyone else is already taken." The question that follows should not be rushed. Be gracious with yourself, knowing that you will make mistakes but that you were not created a mistake. Look into your inner needs and the things you crave—how you feel when you do the things you crave to do or how you feel when you think about doing them. These are all clues to living an "inside out" life, and they lead where the world most needs you to be. Those clues show you why you only need one life to live and not the nine of a cat.

<u>Rediscovery</u>

What activities do you crave doing and would want to do over and over again?

_____
_____
_____
_____
_____
_____
_____

There is as much guidance in way that closes behind us as there is in way that opens up ahead of us. The opening may reveal our potentials while the closing may reveal our limits—two sides of the same coin, the coin called identity.

—Parker Palmer, *Let Your Life Speak*

CHAPTER 6

Not Failure, but Feedback

Society has an aversion to failure. Failure is not acceptable, and when it occurs, we are taught to quickly brush it off and, if at all possible, find fault and blame. When quotes like "98 percent is 2 percent short" are touted as mantras pointing toward excellence, it is no wonder we work at hiding our limitations. But at what point do we concentrate so much on the 2 percent that we forget to be grateful and appreciate the 98 percent? Who wants to be judged solely on the 2 percent?

I get the whole striving for 100 percent and perfection, and believe me, if I were to lie on an operating table in a surgical unit, I'd sure hope the surgeon wouldn't say, "Well, this is probably going to be one of those two percenters"—especially if the anesthetic hadn't quite done its job and had not knocked out my hearing. Why do we view some of our limitations, weaknesses, failures, and shortcomings to such extremes that we become paralyzed in moving forward? The truth is that those pieces of information can serve as a guide to our strengths, potential, and future successes.

When I was a bit younger and had delusional visions of becoming a professional downhill skier, I spent many a weekend on a ski hill close to my home. When you are in that culture and become a regular on the hill, you get to know others, and you pick up on the unspoken hierarchy among downhillers. You soon find out who is "king of the hill," who is just "recreational," and who doesn't "stand a chance in hill" (typo intentional).

On my local hill stood an icon of a man who was admired and respected by all of us. Most of us only knew him by name and reputation, but if he was within eyesight on the same slope, we made an extra effort in our style to impress him. Our intensity would increase. Cuts were crisper and shorter. Tips were held a bit higher and skis a bit closer together. We were vying to be noticed, and we hoped that on one of the following lineups to catch a chair to the top, we would be lucky enough to hear him yell "Single!" And we would push and shove one another, bailing on our friends in the hopes that we would be his next seatmate. Of course, we were hopeful that would lead the conversation into his affirmation of our skill and ultimately lead to his endorsement of our exceptional, phenomenal abilities on the boards.

Looking back, it was pretty hilarious, I guess, if one was simply observing how we would start showing off by dropping hints when he was within earshot. Walter was an idol in our eyes and was worshipped, so we brought him our sacrifices at the altar of the hill every weekend.

Once in a while, everything just aligns for our benefit, and all things are orchestrated for that perfect point in time where we get our chance. One sunny Saturday morning, he looked directly at me, and he bellowed "Single!" I pushed forward with my poles, cut across the top of someone else's skis in front of me, and strode up alongside to catch the next chair. My chance to be impressive and get that nod of approval would become the defining moment that I would be referring to in future interviews for *Sports Illustrated*. I had so much to say and had all the opening lines anyone would ever need for a lifetime, and at that precise moment of sitting on the chair to catch the lift, my brain froze as much as the snow below my skis. I went blank and simply stared straight ahead, paralyzed by my own inabilities to open my mouth. Nothing was said by either one of us for the lower half of the ride up. He would busily wave to skiers below while I was internally freaking out as thoughts of dropping a pole or one ski dropping out of a binding played with my psychosis. Visions of living in Putzville and retiring there was a very real possibility for me at that point. By the time we got to the halfway tower, he had changed his focus from being ambassador on the hill to concentrating on me. "So, how is your day going on the hill?" he asked. I'm pretty sure that is what he asked, but I think what he really meant to say, at least in my mind, was this: "I have seen you all day, and you are one amazing skier. That sharp cut you made in the mogul run was simply spectacular. Never seen it done with such perfection! You made it look so easy and smooth. You should seriously consider a professional career in downhill. If I had your talent, I sure would." So, if my interpretation of his question was correct, I would need to set up my response with some brilliant answer that would woo this downhill god. Feeling the immense pressure of my entire skiing career lying in the hands of this man's opinion, I said, "Great! I didn't even fall once today!" After all, I thought, the true measure of a good skier was that he or she almost never fell, so I was pretty sure I had nailed my response.

I was totally not prepared for two things at that moment: first, the short time we had—only seconds—to prepare to get off the chairlift and down the ramp, and second, his response to my comment. "Ah, that's too bad. Then you didn't learn anything today," he said. And down the ramp he went while I nearly missed the disembarkation process and almost had to make the "ride of shame"—heading down the hill on the chairlift while all others heading up would scoff and jeer at me.

Apparently, not falling does not make you a great skier, and falling does not make you a bad skier. I hated that guy for the remainder of the skiing season. Dream killer! In my mind he was no longer the "king of the hill" but more the old guy who was "over the hill." Years later I realized that not only was he correct, but his words were very wise that day. He told me that making a mistake or two is something to learn from and not something to avoid at all costs. If you are not willing to fail and learn, then you are likely not ready to release your potential because you will be held captive by the comfort zone you create.

I have since failed more times than I can recall. I have tried things that have bombed. I have tried other things through which, after great effort and a never-give-up attitude, little if any success was evident. But in all that lack of success, the really brilliant thing is that I have learned much about my potential and passions by trying. I learned that what in my mind I thought I would love was in reality a bit of a bore that with time became a dislike. Funny how we romanticize a career or job, but soon enough reality shows us our real lack of desire, ability, and capacity to do it for the rest of our lives.

I have also learned that these times keep my expectations reasonable. My perception is my reality, and when my expectations become the measurement I use, they often are unrealistic not only for me but for others as well. We have to test our expectations by trying, and in trying we learn that what we might have thought would be great actually isn't. And in that failure, we get feedback.

I wonder how many times David had to swing that sling around his head and miss the target, maybe even hitting the back of his head with the leather straps. How many different kinds of stones—round, flat, oval, smooth, rough, sharp, or other—did he have to try before knowing exactly what to use for each unique situation? How did he know how far to stand from Goliath in order to lodge a stone in his forehead? I would venture the argument that he had to fail a number of times prior to knowing these things. And so it is with you. If you have walked on this earth for a bit, then you have tasted the sourness of failure. What we need to do is view the aftertaste not as some kind of lingering repulsive flavor that leads us to inaction and paralysis but as a taste that defines our appetite for a new flavor that we crave. It becomes an elimination process as we sort through activities and events that we know lead to discovery of our being and the places of purpose that contain meaning.

Leonard Cohen, in his song "Anthem," puts it beautifully: "Ring the bells that still can ring. Forget the perfect offering. There is a crack in everything. That's how the light gets in."

If you live in North America and have ever gone out to eat at a restaurant, there is a good chance that at least once you were at a smorgasbord. You picked a warm plate from the trolley and went around the islands of food, taking some you liked and passing on the ones that you did not like. How did you know which ones you would like and which ones should not have a chance of touching your plate? You knew the difference because at some point you tried samplings of the foods, and with the help of your taste buds, you determined what you loved and hated. A smorgasbord is a trial-and-error scenario, full of success and failure, full of crave and avoid. In trying and failing, we refine our choices and begin to enjoy our time and experiences. If you were to have a bad experience at the smorgasbord and from that one experience decide to never eat any food ever again, you would starve to death. Failure is feedback, and that feedback helps you understand something about the real you.

In order to truly get to the point where your potential gets released, you need to take an honest look into past limitations and somehow figure out what that feedback is telling you about that activity. Yes, good skiers fall, and yes, 98 percent is 2 percent short of 100. But maybe that 2 percent is crucial in pointing the way. "Yes" is a way, but "no" is a way as well.

Know that *you* are *not* a mistake! You have been wonderfully and uniquely made, and within that there is a beauty and genius possessed by only you in order to carry out your purpose and mission.

Rediscovery

What have past failures provided you in the way of feedback?

_____
_____
_____
_____
_____
_____
_____

I don't want you to know it...I want you to believe it.

—Unknown

CHAPTER 7

What's Belief Got to Do with It?

There is an old story about the famous Zumbrati, who crossed Niagara Falls on a tightrope. That particular day the weather was less than ideal, especially for the stunt he was trying to accomplish safely. The wind was blowing, and Zumbrati was more than thankful when he crossed the raging and deadly waterfall and stood on dry ground on the other side from where he had started.

On that side a man with a wheelbarrow was in line waiting to congratulate him. "I believe you could cross this waterfall pushing this wheelbarrow," he said.

Zumbrati, who at that point had his adrenalin pumping back to a normal rate, simply shook his head in disbelief at the dare that had just been presented to him.

The man was relentless in his urging, "I believe you can do it!" Zumbrati kept declining the offer as graciously as he could, but the hounding continued.

Finally, Zumbrati, with his patience tested to the limit, said, "You really do believe in me, don't you?"

"Oh, I do," the man said convincingly.

"OK," Zumbrati replied. "Get into the wheelbarrow!"

Belief in action. It is good that you believe you can do something, and it must start there, but eventually you will need to act on that belief. Not acting is like a company safety committee that tells its workers this: "Nobody moves—nobody gets hurt." True, but sooner rather than later, all will find themselves unemployed. There has to be an action part to your belief.

Stepping out and taking a risk is the action part of believing in who you are and moving you toward your passion. Passion without action stays a "someday" dream. Someday all I have been waiting for will align, and I will do it. Someday I will finally be asked by my boss to do that job I always dreamed of. Someday I will show them what they don't know I can do. It stops just being a dream when you stop making excuses.

I think our "someday" battle is one of self-doubt, and really we are saying, "What if I really can't do it? What if I fail? What if I get laughed at? What if?"

If you know who you have been created to be, then who cares if they say no? "Being" and "doing" need to be in sync in order for others to see our passion or sweet spot. That's necessary if we desire to release our potential—and not just for others to see but for us to believe.

Having chaired many job-recruitment panels for various companies, I have heard candidates state how passionate they were about this and that (usual they have inserted something directly out of the wording from the job ad). I should actually warn candidates at the start not to go down that road with me unless they have a solid answer backed by proof. I will always challenge anyone about his or her so-called passion if it is not backed by some evidence of action. If you tell me what you believe to be your passion, then I need you to prove it through example. When we see "being" aligned with "doing," we believe.

When people tell me they are passionate about something, what they really are saying is that they like to do a certain thing. They even occasionally say they love it. But when they're pushed on the issue to show it in action and they can't back it up, their statement sounds hollow.

Do yourself one of the biggest favors you can, and align your passions with action. Describe to yourself what your passions mean and what a manifestation of those look like in your life. I want you to know it, but more importantly, I want you to believe it.

Rediscovery

What do you know and what do you believe about your potential and passions that can be proven by your actions?

_____
_____
_____
_____
_____
_____
_____

Light yourself on fire with passion and people will come from miles to watch you burn.

—John Wesley

CHAPTER 8

Two Little Words That Make a Big Difference

There was a difference between Mr. Clarke and Mr. Stan. They held similar positions in the same career, but everyone knew that, given the choice, you'd rather have Mr. Clarke on one of his bad days than Mr. Stan on one of his good days. It was a remarkable difference, and the evidence was overwhelming that the only similarity was in title. They were both teachers in my high school. Although one taught English and the other science, it was not the subject that made us prefer one to the other—both subjects were mandatory. We looked forward to Mr. Clarke's class and would often be sitting in class well before the bell rang. We were calm, eager, and positive. The same could not be said of Mr. Stan's class. We straggled in, sat bleary eyed, and took naps.

It took every ounce of energy to walk into Mr. Stan's classroom. The only one ever on time for Mr. Stan's class was Mr. Stan himself. With slumped shoulders and the avoidance of eye contact, we slunk into our chairs behind the lab tables and slouched for the entire rest of the hour. There were more requests for bathroom breaks and absences than all other classes combined.

It wasn't that Mr. Stan was a particularly bad teacher in the sense of his knowledge, skills, or experience. And on the opposite side, Mr. Clarke was inexperienced, rather new to the trade after years in the military, and as the saying goes, "a little wet behind the ears." They both knew their respective subjects well. Most of society would quickly pass judgment on the two as to their abilities based on length of time teaching, postsecondary educational degree, and any status that came along with the name of the alma mater. Based on that data, an assumption could be made about which teacher would be loved and admired and which one would be avoided and ignored. But it doesn't work that way. There is something that education, title, and status do not give you to guarantee success.

As I sat in class with both teachers and began to observe what was really going on, I noticed that the difference could simply be explained in two little words we use every day but take for granted—*in* versus *into*.

Mr. Stan was *in* a job, and Mr. Clarke was *into* his job. The observable results in the classroom were remarkable.

In can be defined as showing up physically and putting in time—basically satisfied but all in all disengaged.

Into can be defined as showing up physically, mentally, and emotionally—engrossed and checked in, all in all engaged.

One is effective; the other is not.

One is full of energy; the other is not.

One creates excitement; the other does not.

One breathes life; the other sucks it away.

Not only was Mr. Stan only *in* his position, but also, as students, we were only *in* his classroom because we had to be. We were present in body alone for attendance and a passing grade. As for Mr. Clarke's classroom, we were *into* that hour because Mr. Clarke was *into* his subject. We were attentive, and assignments were mostly done on time, and the in-class discussions were harder to end than to start. Even snap quizzes weren't protested like they were in other classes.

There appears to be a direct correlation with how *into* something we are and how *into* something the person we are dealing with is. I am sure if you think back to someone you had dealings with who was merely *in* his or her job, you began a quest to replace that person shortly after the experience. Was it a customer service situation, and you began to shop elsewhere? Perhaps it was a mechanic who reduced your confidence in the work done. Maybe it was a dentist or doctor who caused you to ask around for recommendations from friends and family.

Have you ever watched a married couple at a restaurant? You can tell just by observation which couples are merely *in* their marriage and the ones who are still *into* their relationship. There is a big difference in attention to each other and their level of engagement as they enjoy or don't enjoy the company of each other.

How about that barista pouring your morning coffee—*in* or *into* the job? Which one would you prefer to keep going back to time and time again? Why? I can tell you that you are likely to simply tolerate the one *in* the job who serves you the coffee, but the one who is *into* the position will make the coffee taste better. And the conversation you are likely to have with the latter will likely be as good for you in the morning as the caffeine jolt your body craves.

So up to this point in this chapter, I have been accusing others of being *in* or *into*. What about you? What does that look like personally for you?

A clue to where your potential can be released lies within the things you are *into*. Being *into* something provides you with the greatest opportunity for you to be the very best you possibly can be; the growth within that area is almost limitless. If you are just *in* the activity, you are limited to how far you can go. Watch any sports team in the playoffs, and you can witness the hunger and passionate focus in what they are trying to accomplish. Not all championship teams are made of the best-skilled players. Watch a team that is trying to get the coach fired (yes, it happens), and you will see a team that is made up of skilled players simply *in* the game, with potential not being released.

Rob Gilbert, in the booklet *Bits & Pieces*, put it this way: "Being IN something does not mean you will get anything out of it. The only way you will ever get the most out of it is if you are totally INTO it."

To be truly passionate about something means you are *into* it. Of course, there will be parts of your life that you will only be *in*—things that you perhaps have skills and abilities for but that fail to create a fire within. Some things are necessary parts of everyday life, like paying bills, feeding and clothing yourself and others, and so forth. The problem begins when *all* you are ever doing is made up of these tasks, and your days are filled with only satisfying the very basic of needs. I call them "tasks" because even the sound of the word carries the tone of drudgery and monotony. Have you noticed how interchangeable the words "tasks" and "chores" seem to be? Have you heard anyone doing work in his or her area of passion ever refer to that work as a chore or task?

The goal cannot be to fully eliminate the parts of your life that require a certain number of tasks—that is impossible to do. The goal is to identify what you are *into* and what you are merely *in*, and then begin to manage them accordingly to release all the potential you have within. And when you get to that point of identifying and managing the small things you are *in*, they don't seem to be as big a deal as you once thought. Instead, they become a small hurdle you can easily leap over, and you no longer view them as that large brick wall you once made them out to be.

If you truly want to get to that point where you are "being" authentically what you are craving to become, you will need to take stock of the activities you are just *in* and the ones you are *into*, and then begin to lean more and more of your time toward the latter. Before you fill out the next rediscovery question, remember that we are not referring here to a noun—a person, place, or thing—but a verb, which is an action, something you are doing.

Rediscovery

Make a list of *activities* you can clearly place in each column.

IN	INTO
•	•
•	•
•	•
•	•
•	•
•	•
•	•
•	•
•	•
•	•
•	•
•	•

**There are places you survive and
places where you thrive.**

—**Anonymous**

CHAPTER 9

More or Less

How often do you ask someone a question hoping for a precise response, and you hear in response, "More or less"?

What kind of answer is that? It could be just one of my pet peeves, but I hate that answer. My dislike for that response is never more evident than when I chair a panel interview for job candidates. The answer "more or less" does nothing to pole-vault that person into the lead for the position. Exactly at the point when the person has the opportunity to shine the brightest light on his or her potential or passion, the light flickers like a bulb that is totally underpowered. The sense of confidence one gets from that answer is anything but strong.

"More or less!" It is speaking imprecisely and is synonymous with "approximately," "roughly," "nearly," "almost," "close to," or "round about." How does that instill any understanding for others to gauge desire and potency?

OK, I will cut you some slack for using that phrase from time to time if you have to guess about figures or statistics, but you do not do yourself any favors in touting your potential when you use terms like that to describe your likes and dislikes—the things that engage your attention and those that disengage the whole of you.

Q: "Do you like to meet strangers and find out more about them?"
A: "More or less."
Q: "Would you rather spend time with an old acquaintance or someone new?"
A: "More or less."
Q: "Do you enjoy long periods of staying focused on one task with many details?"
A: "More or less."
Q: "Do you like starting new projects?"
A: "More or less."

Do you see what I mean? A response like that provides no insight into your potential and the opportunities that may release it. Staying entirely neutral like that is like straddling a white picket fence with one leg on either side. If the fence is low enough, basically you get away with it, but if the fence is high and it really matters, you are eventually going to feel some pain, and it will be self-inflicted and needless.

The individuals I see who are among the most satisfied and secure never use "more or less" when describing themselves. They are precise in their personal understanding, or better put, they are fully aware of specifics around what they need more of and what they need less of in their world. And with this understanding, they begin to craft and manage a life around their potential, passions, and purpose. There is a *but* to this, however, and here it is: *but* they had to consciously stop and think about the activities that engaged them, the activities they looked forward to, and the ones they hoped to repeat sooner than later. It does not stop there. They also seriously considered which activities they disengaged from, which activities they did not look forward to doing, and which activities generated negative thoughts at the prospect of repetition. In other words, and simply put, what activities did they want more and more of in their day, and what activities did they want less and less of? The really amazing thing about these folks is that over time they slowly began to steer their careers around those two boundaries. It does not happen overnight. It takes time. I never view it as "just a lucky break" for them. They may say that they caught a lucky break, but when you dig deeper, you realize that they worked for quite some time in crafting and positioning themselves for a particular opportunity. We outside observers, of course, just see the end result and forget all about the years of hard work that went into what we see them doing.

It all starts with honesty and self-discovery to the core. And in that core, the discovery tends not to be some large global statement about an activity but refined details around particular activities. Instead of stating that they enjoy project work, they go into more detail with precision of what kinds of projects, with whom they want to partner, and even the specific and intricate parts of a project that they are best at.

I love starting a new project or being part of a new start. When it evolves to where minute details are necessary and those details become the bulk of the task, I check out. I can't help myself. I just lose all interest in that part of the process, and I start looking for the next project to get started. This was an important discovery in my understanding of myself. When I find places to lean into that utilize my enthusiasm and energy in getting things into a start-up phase where success is likely to occur, you will not only see the best of me, but you will also get the fullness of my potential being released. Knowing I can easily release confidence in others who are masters of the world of details ensures engagement and success not only for me but also for others involved in the project. Knowing this also frames boundaries for my involvement or noninvolvement around activities. I have learned over time how to best manage and navigate requests for involvement in projects. I ask questions like the following: How long will the project take? What am I responsible for? Who else is part of this, and what do they bring to the team? Can I do what I do best and walk away knowing with confidence others are continuing on with the details to see it through to the end?

Looking back at my history, I see even as a kid I craved those things—whether it was in a classroom project or early in my working career. I see examples of times when that happened and almost everyone was successful—of course, with the help of others doing their part. When I was saddled with a project from start to finish all on my own and bogged down in the details, it often did not end well, or the suffering lasted longer than it should have. I am not saying that I am in some sense irresponsible, because I truly am committed to success and hate to see good projects fail; I just know exactly where I will be engaged and where not—where success is likely or not likely to occur. There comes a freedom in being able to say no in the same way there is freedom in saying yes.

Those kinds of discoveries for you are a key to finding out what your potential, passions, and purpose are as you journey toward being and not just doing—where you will thrive by being *into* and not just strive while being *in*.

Do yourself a favor, and discover some specifics about the activities you need more of and those you need less of. Once you know this, the process of managing them is easier and leads to more contentment and success.

Caution 1: When determining what you need more of, do not just think of those things that you are naturally good at, but also think of the things that engage, energize, and encourage you to want to do them again and again.

Caution 2: When determining what you need less of, look to the things that disengage, deflate, and discourage you from wanting to repeat doing them again, not just the things you consider yourself to be bad at. Get down to the details as they pertain to the activity.

Rediscovery

What activities do you need more of, and what activities do you need less of?

MORE	LESS
•	•
•	•
•	•
•	•
•	•
•	•
•	•
•	•
•	•
•	•

"My dear boy," Miss Frost said sharply. "My dear boy, please don't put a label on me—don't make me a category before you get to know me!"

John Irving, *In One Person*

CHAPTER 10

Excuse Me, but Your Label Is Sticking Out

Like most people, you are likely resistant to walking up to a stranger and mentioning a stuck-out clothes label to the person. You try to avoid looking at it, but it is right there, and you can't help yourself. You may even be hopeful that someone else will mention it so that you don't have to. It is so obvious to everyone but the person with the problem. The closeness of the relationship with this person will determine the likelihood of mentioning it. If you are close and feel comfortable pointing it out, you simply say, "Excuse me, but your label is sticking out." You may even add, "Here, let me fix it for you."

Funny how we do that and feel like we are going to offend the person, yet we appreciate it when others point out such a thing for us. The kindness of that gesture is appreciated by most of us.

Most garment labels are sewn on the inside for only the owner to refer to. A typical label provides the owner with all the user information necessary regarding the origin, authenticity, size, materials used, care instructions, and possible warnings. It is like a tiny owner's manual all printed on an impossible-to-read square piece of cloth sewn into the garment where it tends to be the itchiest.

We humans tend to have something in common with the garment label. We too have care instructions and handling instructions attached to us, some of which are of our own doing and many of which are the labels others place upon us from observation, perception, and stereotyping.

I wonder if you have ever viewed those descriptive labels as a possible clue to who you really are and where you may actually have some hidden potential—potential that, if released productively, could lead you into a passion you have.

Let me provide a couple of personal examples. Most of my life I have been accused of looking for the shortcuts in either doing something or going somewhere. At times the labels I wore around this trait were self-doubt and a bit of shame. I just couldn't help but see a quicker and more efficient way of doing things. I easily and quickly could eliminate clutter and chaos that lay in front of me. Seeing multiple options, I would quickly discard unnecessary steps or paths to making a decision.

This skill (as I refer to it now) was likely what got me into trouble at school with my teachers. It just made absolutely no sense in my head why one would take ten steps to solve a math problem when the answer could be found in six steps. My report cards often reflected and provided feedback to my parents that missing a step or two in the process of solving math problems wasn't worthy of a passing grade. I was accused of cheating or guessing the answers. I remember one math class where I failed the final exam, which would have allowed me to pass the course and never ever take another math class in my life. I got one problem marked wrong even though I had the correct answer. I was told that I did not show my work in the exact steps the teacher had taught. Even though the answer was correct, it was marked incorrect, causing me to fail the class and forcing a repeat of taking the subject. Ouch! I grew up thinking that shortcuts in the eyes of others were wrong. That led to self-doubt, and frankly, I was sure something was wrong with me. It wasn't until later in life, when one employer in particular saw something else in me, that I began to see the possible value of my skill in this area. It no longer was a negative but a positive. I was able to find efficiencies in the system of coordinating the company's process of client intake. I showed them possible alternatives and the consequences of each possibility and recommended the best option. It was a label not to hide anymore but one to wear outside with confidence. It's a skill I use every day in business—and it was sitting there the whole time.

The second label I wore and suppressed was that I was apparently fussy and a nitpicker. The kinder word would be "perfectionist." You likely wouldn't notice that about me on first impression, but if you got to know me a bit, you would notice that "good enough" isn't a statement I resonate well with. I prefer something to be "great!" Now, that isn't in every aspect in my life, but it does exist in enough areas that it may drive the odd person crazy, especially when I point out what would make a good thing even better. I figured out that I could see the greatness of some potential, especially in people. This realization started when I worked with prison inmates who were about to be released from their incarceration. The program was to help reduce recidivism through gainful employment. What others saw as hopeless cases, I saw mostly as individuals with potential and pure genius. I thought I was going crazy until it was pointed out to me by a friend that what I saw was the good in others. If we could tap into that potential and shift our perception slightly, we might actually be able to help make a difference. All that potential channeled in a way to generate more life could cause positive outcomes versus the negative outcomes these inmates were used to. Our world continues to be fascinated with what is wrong and weak, but that's the wrong fascination.

The labels others place on you actually describe the potential you possess. They are positives and not negatives that others believe you to be. I now look for opportunities where I can assist people and organizations to efficiently find alternative strategies and make something or someone better. I now wear these two labels—efficiency maker and perfectionist—with a sense of purpose rather than something to hide.

Read the list that follows, and see if any of the terms refer to you. Or see if you have described a coworker or loved one that way. This is by no means a complete list, but it's a short one to give you the basic sense that every negative label carries with it a positive alternative when used to generate more life.

NEGATIVE	MIGHT BE	POSITIVE
Fence-Sitter	might be	Harmonious
Disorganized	might be	Creative
Stubborn	might be	Dedicated
Shy	might be	Reflective
Unrealistic	might be	Positive
Negative	might be	Realistic
Indecisive	might be	Adaptable
Arrogant	might be	Confident
Anal	might be	Thorough
Inflexible	might be	Consistent
Cautious	might be	Deliberative
Rigid	might be	Disciplined

Intense	might be	Focused
Dreamer	might be	Visionary
Pollyanna	might be	Positive
Micromanager	might be	Responsible

Remember that someone's perception is that person's reality. By wearing our labels on the outside and telling people what those labels really mean, we can begin to change people's perceptions so that they're closer to the truth. A label is steeped in the perceptions of others, and before long we begin to believe those impressions as the truth. Once that happens, we begin to use these labels as barriers and excuse generators, and excuses prevent us from doing the very things we could and should do.

"We inhabit a world in which we tend to put labels on one another and expect that we will then march through life wearing them like permanent sandwich boards."

—Nick Webb

Rediscovery

Make your own list of labels you have carried and what they truly mean.

NEGATIVE Barrier label Perception Excuse	IS	POSITIVE Potential Reality Action
	Is	
	Is	
	Is	
	Is	
	Is	
	Is	
	Is	
	Is	
	Is	
	Is	
	Is	
	Is	
	Is	
	Is	
	Is	
	Is	

Yes no yes no yes no?
Red blue?
Yes red, no blue?
No red, yes no?
In out, up down?
Do don't, can can't?
Choices sit on the shelf life
New shoes in a shoe shop.
If the in crowd are squeezing into a must-have shoe
And the one pair left are too tiny for you
Don't feel compelled into choosing them
If you're really a size 9, buy that size.
While everyone else
Hobbles around with sore feet
Your choices should feel comfortable
Or they aren't your choices at all
Why limp when you can sprint?

David Baird, *Fiesta of Happiness: Be True To Yourself*

CHAPTER 11
Size Does Matter

The older I get, the more and more I am convinced that most changes that have an impact on our daily lives are not large and sudden events but small events, small decisions, and small adjustments. It is the smaller things combined that make the appearance of sudden change and noticeable movements.

My thinking appears to be in good company if you have read Malcolm Gladwell's book *Tipping Point*. He builds the case that ideas, products, messages, and even behaviors spread like a virus—with small things connecting into large movements. He says that "in order to create one contagious movement, you often have to create many small movements first."

I have spent many hours working with many restless individuals who are on a quest seeking passion and purpose. They almost all begin with the belief that the next step necessary in the process is a huge life-changing career change. Often little thought is given to the multitude of consequences and the destructive wake that may leave. They believe the only solution left is a massive overhaul. Most have had long careers in some industry, and they are ready to toss them to the side in the hopes that the present shackles they feel will be released and that they will finally reach the utopian world of total fulfillment. Whether they are tired, bored, unchallenged, frustrated, or burned out, they all grasp onto the thought of a massive one-time, life-altering change. A few have come to this idea because of some kind of personal health reason or a family matter that required a large change of this magnitude but that was often out of their control. The majority of the disillusioned have reached a level in their careers that has somehow strangled their potential advancement, responsibility level, or sense of belonging and community.

I am always a bit shocked at how large a change they think they need to make in one instant. They are ready to throw their entire history on the junk pile without even the slightest thought of recycling it. I will admit at times the thought is very sexy and adventurous, but it seldom holds much success in reality. Our human systems are just not designed to take that kind of shock other than in our fantasies and the homemade movies we star in that replay over and over in our minds. Why did we long ago dream of what we have finally become and now wish to discard it completely and exchange it for something with even less possibility of success and happiness?

"We have, in short, somehow become convinced that we need to tackle the whole problem, all at once. But the truth is that we don't. We only need to find the stickiness Tipping Points," says Gladwell.

Here are my findings, not built on a scientific survey or some mathematical algorithm but based in reality through conversations and observations. At least 90 percent of those who come to me with the notion of a massive career change eventually conclude they are in the right career and industry. Through some deep soul work and self-discovery, they realize that what was burning inside them years ago still has a glowing ember. What once was a crackling fire has perhaps lost its glow and warmth, but it isn't extinguished completely. All they needed to do to reignite the fire of passion within was to make some small changes and decisions to better align with their present situation and desires. Some have gone astray by chasing more money or more status or by trying to meet unrealistic expectations of themselves or others. Getting back to who they are and finding that purpose again has made the difference—without discarding their education, experience, and influence. And when they get to that realization, they express in a sense of surprise and gratitude how it wasn't one big thing but the small decisions, perceptions, or shifts in duties, responsibilities, location, or boundaries that were the reigniting agents.

Let me show you what I mean. I recently had the opportunity to work with a leader of a very large organization that had a number of satellite offices spread over a large geographical area. The leader I was working with was frustrated to the point of almost resigning and thinking a whole new unfamiliar industry was the best viable option. As we began to converse, we began to uncover the source of most his discontent at work, which frankly was spilling over into his personal life.

In order to become more efficient and control some costs that had gotten out of control, the head office had mandated that he hold, and be responsible for, weekly meetings via the telephone with all his satellite managers. It had come to be known by all as "the call," and not in a positive tone. He bemoaned the regular Friday afternoon calls, referring to them as "unproductive bitch sessions" in which everyone was preoccupied with getting the last of the week's work completed before the long and strenuous commute home. He knew this because most of what he heard was the pounding of keyboards in the background and obligatory "ahas," "I sees," and "sures!" And when the conversation was opened to any of their thoughts, it was always around the negatives of the week, consisting of goals and targets that were not met, all coated in a shroud of blame and excuses. After a couple of years with this weekly dread of his, he seriously entertained not a subtle move but one huge career change. When he finally hit the level of frustration that he could barely cope any longer, he got desperate. It was clearly evident that he was fantasizing about a new adventure. In essence, he was contemplating rather seriously having a new role in a new position in an unfamiliar industry. He was about to cheat on himself.

We talked about the reality of such an action and what could be gained or lost by acting on such an impulse. We talked about the source of his frustrations and visualized what a completely new industry might look like for him. And then, without any premeditation on my part, I asked what I thought to be a simple and innocent question. "Why do you hold these meetings on a Friday afternoon when it sounds like everyone is busy tying up loose ends to get away for the weekend? He replied quickly, "Head office told us."

Two things instantly occurred to him when he heard his answer out loud. First, he realized he was making excuses and blaming others just like the managers on the Friday calls were blaming him. Second, he heard for the first time that he may have some choice in the matter that he had never thought of, because he had made an assumption that the meetings had to be done late in the afternoon on Fridays. He followed it up with this statement: "Fridays are the worst days for us to do calls. Instead of talking about targets we met, we talk about everything that went wrong in the week. Who likes to hear that all the time? It is a complete downer for the entire team, and we dread Friday afternoons."

It was at that instant that he grabbed his smartphone and blasted out an e-mail to all his managers relating to that next week and for the foreseeable future: the Friday calls would be changed to early Tuesday mornings, and all participants needed to clear that time off their calendars for the weekly call.

One month later we talked again. I told him I was surprised to hear from him because when his number appeared on my call display, I was wondering if it was his voice on the phone or his replacement. He chuckled a bit and then stated in a more enthusiastic tone than I had ever heard in any of our previous conversations, "Changing those calls to a Tuesday has made all the difference in my week. Everyone is attentive, blaming is minimized, complaining comes with suggested solutions, and we look at what we want to accomplish for the week. And the best thing, I don't hear keyboards in the background anymore—I had no idea how that noise drove me crazy."

"So, you still looking for a whole new career?" I asked.

"Nope. It isn't perfect, but no job is, and I know I am in the right career. I cannot believe how something so little was the change I needed." From what I understand, he continues to journey with the same company to this day.

I realize as you read this that it sounds too simple that everyone lives happily ever after, but you might just be amazed how a very small thing can change a big thing. So I guess size does matter. Big isn't always better or even the solution. Small is powerful, and when the small events begin to connect and collide in unison, the rest of us stand back and say, "Wow! That was a big step." But it wasn't; it just appeared that it was. Movements that cause change are made up of many smaller pieces that have united to appear larger than they really are.

Rediscovery

What small things are driving you crazy that you might have the power to adjust to have a positive impact on how you do your work?

_____
_____
_____
_____
_____
_____
_____

Give me six hours to chop down a tree and I will likely spend the first four sharpening the axe.

—Abraham Lincoln

CHAPTER 12

Straight A's

You likely know of, have met, or are one of those people who has the distinction of getting straight A's in school. That simple designation requires no definition to all of us who have spent any time in school getting grades and report cards. Everyone knows the meaning of that phrase. I know the meaning, but certainly not from personal attainment.

In addition to all of us knowing personally one of these people, we may also have watched a movie or two in which one of the characters in the story played the role of the straight-A student. We, along with the rest of the cast, refer to such a student in other terms: brainiac, bookworm, teacher's pet. With these terms comes a stereotype of little or no social life, skimpy skill in athletics, social awkwardness, and serving as a target for all kinds of practical jokes, including locker stuffing. But come final exam time, that student suddenly becomes everyone's best friend, at least temporarily.

When it comes to those I have had the privilege of working with who have figured out and discovered their true potential, passions, and purpose, they all have something in common with the straight-A student.

They incorporate straight A's into their lives as well. They have become successful at the discovery of self and of others. The Gallup organization has done amazing research and work in this field around strengths, and I encourage you to check it out. What I share in this chapter is an adaptation of Gallup's work, but I do want to give Donald Clifton and Gallup the credit due to their great work with over seventy years of research in positive psychology.

In order, the sequence of five A's that I like to get individuals to complete are awareness, acceptance, appreciation, application, and alignment. Skipping any step in the sequence will lead to some missed discoveries and incompleteness. There are no shortcuts, so give yourself some time and grace as you go through this chapter. You may even find it beneficial to ask others you trust to assist you in this part of your discovery.

Awareness

One definition of awareness: having or showing realization, perception, or knowledge.

Alternative definition: an honest realization of who I am, what activities make me come alive, knowing my limits, and thinking back to the things that always were this way.

Acceptance

One definition of acceptance: the quality or state of being accepted.

Alternative definition: coming to terms with acceptance of the truth that you are uniquely designed and have potential, passions, and purpose that may look different than those of others. Being able to confidently describe your strengths and weaknesses, potentials and limitations, likes and dislikes, and cravings and distastes.

Appreciation

One definition of appreciation: the ability to understand the worth, quality, or importance of something.

Alternative definition: a gratefulness for what, who, why, and where you are at your best in addition to understanding that others working together make a family, community, and team well rounded, and that well-roundedness can't apply to you alone.

Application

One definition of application: the act of putting to use either a new technique or new application for an old remedy.

Alternative definition: taking your new discoveries and rediscoveries and applying them with a new perspective, which may require some trial and error for confirmation.

Alignment

One definition of alignment: the proper positioning or state of adjustment of the parts in relation to one another.

Alternative definition: the sweet spot of where being is doing, and they are aligned so that discovering your potential leads to developing your passions, which leads to determining your purpose.

The old adage that you need to crawl before you run is the principle behind this assignment and the stages of this development. Yes, it takes time. Yes, it takes patience. Yes, it takes some risk. But when fully aligned and when all stages have been thoughtfully and honestly wrestled with, one becomes fully engaged, and potential, passions, and purpose align into confidence and assurance.

So here is your opportunity to complete for yourself the five A's and move toward that alignment you long for so that being and doing are synchronized.

Rediscovery

Fill in the blanks as they apply to you personally.

Awareness: What have you discovered about your potential and passions?

Acceptance: What do you accept now about yourself and proudly take ownership of?

Appreciation: How are you grateful for your strengths and weaknesses?

Application: Where are you presently applying some of your strengths?

Alignment: Where do you need to position yourself to be offering more?

We cannot be sure of having something to live for unless we are willing to die for it.

—Ernesto Che Guevara

CHAPTER 13

Treasure Hunting

I heard a good friend of mine (Tim), who makes a living doing and being his passion, once say, "In order to be successful in a treasure hunt, you need three things: first, recognize the value of the treasure; second, refuse to settle for anything less, and third, risk everything to possess it."

Much of this book to this point has been on accepting that you have some very real and true strengths, desires, and potential within you. Some you use unconsciously every day, some you may have forgotten about and lie dormant, and some you have never defined as treasure—you just figured everyone has them because they are so natural to who you already are. Identifying and becoming aware is an important process toward "being."

When you get the opportunity to watch truly successful individuals apply their craft and share their inner treasures, you see an ease and beauty of what they do because you are observing potential that is being released. The most successful, no matter how you study it, know what they do best, and they do it as often as possible. They also know what they are not good at and manage around those areas of their lives. It is not about ignoring our limitations; it's about understanding them and not allowing the limitations to control and rule like a ball and chain. And it's about experiencing the freedom of understanding and about beginning to manage those limitations.

Becoming aware of the treasure that lies within is a crucial step. Much like a treasure map for treasure hunters, X marks the spot. Understanding the value is helpful in determining the amount of effort on your part that is necessary to begin ownership. Determining the value begins with the appreciation and acceptance of what the treasure truly is and isn't. Until that part of the process is done—with honesty and a sense of being steeped in authentic reality rather than our own insecurities or overinflated egos—we will be unable to possess and share our treasure with the world.

Risk everything to possess it. Can that be true? Is risk really involved in leaning into your passion? In the case of potential, passions, and purpose, you need to utilize a different term than "risk." Perhaps "sacrifice" is a more accurate word. Charles Dickens said, "The important thing is this: to be ready at any moment to sacrifice what you are for what you could become." If you are serious about releasing your potential, which leads you to your passions and ultimately leads you to your purpose, it will cost you. My conversations and observations led me to believe this. I also believe that most of us let passion die when the costs become evident. The result is we settle into a life of the daily grind otherwise referred to as "the rut." Passions leading to purpose have to be active and sacrificial to be real.

Those who appear to be truly living in their passions experience ownership of the treasure, and in addition, they have had to sacrifice something to get it—time, money, luxuries, lifestyle, social relationships, recognition, and acceptance. And the truth is that it is likely more than just one thing that is costly. Could this be why so few of us actually live our passions and fulfill our purpose?

I have yet to meet anyone who has successfully navigated through the deep waters of finding his or her true purpose who has not had to struggle through the waves of self-doubt and at times the storms of questioning his or her sanity.

Here are just a few examples of what sacrifice could be involved when you are becoming what you could be and not what you presently are.

Take the example of the young First Nations gal who was the first of her indigenous Canadian people on the entire reserve on which she lived to not only graduate from a university with a degree in law but also be the first to even complete high school. She had to sacrifice relationships and undergo taunting about predicted failure from her family and those closest to her. It cost her social relationships as she stayed in her room to study while others with less to lose went out to parties and social events. She had to endure the awkwardness of feeling like she did not belong in her own community as she was seen not as an upcoming shining star but as one who might make the rest look bad—she was shunned. But today, she proudly works in her field, representing and fighting for the equality of the First Nations people in the judicial system. She is a voice for the unheard.

Then there is the beautiful lady who spends many days crossing to the other side of our planet to work with a village in Africa where young girls of a certain tribe are not accepted into the school system and appear to be destined to a life of poverty. It costs her money to travel and to buy supplies. It costs her even more to pay for each of those young girls to get an education that just might make a huge difference to the girl and her future household. She risks her life every time as she heads into a poverty-stricken area and is seen as a rich white person. She spends weeks at a time foregoing the luxuries of a comfortable bed in North America for the chance to sleep restless nights in a dingy excuse for a hotel riddled with who knows what. She risks the pain of grieving when she learns that one of her dearly beloved has been raped, beaten up, or even killed. Helping and building opportunities for individuals to get the same opportunities, she celebrates the success of the outcast. She stands for justice in an unjust system.

What about the middle-aged fellow who, when not working his day job, is spending his evenings and weekends pouring water at the football practices and games of his city's junior football team? It costs him time that he could be spending on himself. It costs him money when one of the players needs a bit to make ends meet or be forced to quit the team and head back home. It costs him his own resources to travel with the team for out-of-town games. All this, and the guy doesn't even understand the game of football. But he does understand the importance of these young lives and the need for mentoring and coaching in all the elements of life that are not football. And when he pours some water or Gatorade, he begins to make that connection and build relationships that sometimes are missing off the field and away from the game. He stands to guide and support young future leaders.

And then there is the male nurse who uses his vacation time to jump on a ship that anchors somewhere in a port where the residents have little or no access to medical help. It costs him his personal vacation time when he could be lying on some beach recharging his body. But he is in more need of recharging his soul, and this is the place he needs to be in order to do that. It costs him financially to get to wherever it is that the ship anchors. It costs him emotionally when he sees that not everyone in need will be served, and some get turned away. It costs him some family time when he is away for the weeks of what he calls giving. He stands for the poor and sick to gain some medical attention that all have a basic right to receive.

Speak to any of these people, and you will hear a wistfulness and quiet confidence that they are not only living up to their potential but also that they are pursuing their passions with purpose. Each one will tell you that it is not always easy and that the costs have made them question the sanity of the decision, but not one would trade it to be what he or she once was. When you cross over to what your passion has released within you from what you once were when that passion lay dormant in the fear of sacrifice, there is no turning back, and you have found your purpose. Rarely will you find someone with passion who has not experienced struggle.

The really amazing thing in most stories I hear is that many live their passions and purpose outside of the daily job they are doing, the place where they get paid and spend many of their daily hours. Each one has come to peace with the idea that his or her job is a means to an end and not the final life chapter being written. For these people, that which once was a quest for their job to be their purpose has been reframed so that the job is simply a vehicle that gets them there. Dig a bit deeper, and you begin to see a direct correlation between much of what they are passionate about and where they are most sacrificial, and that is manifested within their daily work as well; it's just that the outcome looks a bit different. Their purpose is more than a job title or label.

The water boy mentors those he supervises at work as well. The nurse cares for patients at his hometown hospital. The lawyer represents her own reservation and community for free outside of her normal practice. And the woman who gets girls an education in an impoverished land comes home and champions others to come alongside and help gather their efforts as she teaches them the realities of a different world.

It begs the question each of us must grapple with: Do my passion and purpose have to be my job, or does my job allow me the opportunities to release my purposes elsewhere? Is my identity a job title or what I do that produces life in me and others?

I have no doubt that one day I will see all of these people having the opportunity to lean more and more into doing their mission. Much like David versus Goliath, they are presently learning how to slay the giant with a sling while they are shepherding a small flock of sheep. They heard the call and moved toward the giant.

Rediscovery

What sacrifices will it take for you to truly be in your passion and fulfill your purpose?

_____
_____
_____
_____
_____
_____

I have passed through fire and deep water, since we parted. I have forgotten much that I thought I knew, and learned much that I had forgotten.

—J. R. R. Tolkien, *Lord of the Rings*

CHAPTER 14

Your Turn

And so we find ourselves now at the point of getting at the square root of who we are and cycling back to the three questions I started with at the introduction of this book: Who am I? How do I belong? Where can I have the greatest impact?

My understanding of good journalism is that it is the kind that asks the five Ws: who, what, where, when, and why. Take that formula into the equation of the square root of you, and it would appear like this:

Who am I? (Potential = Who?)
What do I love to do? (Passion = Belong?)
Where can I do it? (Passion = Belong?)
When can I use it most? (Passion = Belong?)
Why is it so important to me? (Purpose= Impacting?)

Tracking back through the previous chapters and looking at your answers to the rediscovery questions, you will find that when strung together in a larger narrative, they will give you the answers to the core of your potential, passions, and purpose. You may need to write and rewrite a couple of times to find the answers that best describe you. Reading them over each month will serve as a personal coaching session for you and remind you of the important things that will keep you focused in your pursuit.

The greatest gift you can give this world is to be the real you and to allow others to be the authentic individuals they are. So do everyone a favor, and rediscover the square root of who you are; it's the number that when multiplied by itself gives you the original number. In other words, the square root is the part of you that when multiplied releases all the potential, passions, and purpose of who you have been created to be. You are an original.

The next few pages are blank right now, and I encourage you to fill up the pages with words or pictures or phrases or quotes or whatever it is that best expresses the essence of what we need to know about you. Rediscover what has always been there.

As J. R. R. Tolkien wrote in *The Lord of the Rings*, "He drew a deep breath. 'Well, I'm back,' he said."

Rediscovery

Appendix 1 will provide a small example of what this may look like.

The square root of me is…

_____

_____

_____

_____

_____

_____

_____

RON SCHLITT

RON SCHLITT

SAMPLE NARRATIVE

I love new projects and opportunities where I can be part of a team that sorts through possibilities to find the best ways to move forward. Inviting me into a room with a blank whiteboard will get the very best out of my ability to generate ideas and alternatives. I am most creative in new places with new faces. I naturally look for the story inside of the story and can often see more than one side of a situation. My enthusiasm in starting projects can get the fire started in others before I move on to the next project, and I let others work with the details as I cheer them forward to success. I am best at projects and assignments that are fluid and changing but have a definite deadline.

I have always had the ability to build trust with others, which allows me to see into the dynamics of how others can function effectively. I need solid people with open and curious minds, but I have little patience for drama that undermines the efforts of others. I hate excuses that are generated and played over and over by the same people. I value gratitude.

My talent in seeing how something good can be even better allows me to speak into people and their projects, helping them to realize not only who they are but what they have to give. I love to inspire others with hope for what the future could be.

My potential is serving among others at work, at home, and in my community. My greatest passions are for the underdog and disenfranchised. My purpose is to assist and initiate personal change in others through clarity and hope. This means I need to intentionally carve out time every day to find opportunities where I can sit and listen to others, ask some questions, reflect, listen again, and ask more questions.

ACKNOWLEDGMENTS

Writing a book is never a solo endeavor, and the DNA of many make up the content, stories, and finished product. Many have had an influence in this project—either knowingly or in many cases unknowingly, and I want to express my gratitude for their assistance.

To my greatest cheerleaders, Dianne, Jory, and Jayme—none of this would have been possible without your encouragement, unconditional love, prodding, and teasing. My world would be a lonely place without you three. Thank you! Thank you! Thank you!

Thanks to Tim, David, and Phil—the refiners of thought and prose. Your willingness to hear my scattered thoughts and share your insight and wisdom helped me focus this into something understandable. It is truly a gift you gave me. I am indebted!

My friends at Third Space Life Charity deserve a round of applause. Ken and Linda intentionally create spaces where individuals can experience faith, hope, and purpose. They sacrifice time, talents, and treasure because they believe that tomorrow can be better than today for everyone. Keep being authentic, guys!

Credit must be given to the many who have journeyed before me and pioneered the way toward a strength-based philosophy (far too many to name, but you know who you are). You have all inspired us and made the world a better place because of your research and original thought. I am in awe!

A final thank you to each of you who have embraced the challenge of rediscovering *you*! There is no one like you, so get out and share yourself with the world. We need you!

SUGGESTED RESOURCES

Buckingham, Marcus & Donald O. Clifton. 2001. *Now Discover Your Strengths*. Gallup Press

Gladwell, Malcolm. 2013. *David and Goliath*. Little, Brown and Company

Gladwell, Malcolm. 2000. *Tipping Point*. Back Bay Books

McManus, Erwin Raphael. 2006. *Soul Cravings*. Nelson Books

Palmer, Parker. 1999. *Let Your Life Speak*. Jossey-Bass

Rath, Tom. 2007. *StrengthsFinder 2.0*. Gallup Press

Made in United States
Troutdale, OR
07/31/2023

11704515R00066